GIANCARLO IMPIGLIA
PAINTINGS FOR THE QUEENS
& COLLECTED WORKS

TO ANN CHWATSKY

A FABULOUS

PHOTOGRAPHER

AND A GOOD

FRIEND

[signature]

OCT. 5, 2014

GIANCARLO IMPIGLIA

PAINTINGS FOR THE QUEENS
& COLLECTED WORKS

Introduction by
Christopher Impiglia

Frontispiece:
Portrait of Queen Victoria as a Young Woman, 2007
Pastel on board, 26" x 36"

Previous page:
Self Portrait, 1958
Oil on canvas, 24" x 34"

Giancarlo Impiglia: Paintings for the Queens & Collected Works © 2012 Lily Publications Ltd.

ISBN: 978-1-907945-20-5

Published by:
Lily Publications Ltd
PO Box 33
Ramsey
Isle of Man
IM99 4LP
Telephone +44 (0) 1624 898446

www.lilypublications.co.uk

ACKNOWLEDGEMENT

For me, art is a sublime illusion and artists must hold on to their illusion in order to produce their work. For the artist it is a necessity to maintain their identity, style, and vision, expressing this with a sense of continuity without the influence of fashionable trends. Despite this, in art, as in every human activity, creativity mixed with the desire to succeed induces the artist to gravitate towards the successful trends of the moment. Unfortunately, this attitude causes art to meld with conformity, which in today's art world, is generally accepted.

For more than four decades I have been detaching myself from conformity, creating art by embracing a unique vision where eclecticism is the foundation of my signature style. Within my vision people can identify the influence of the many historically important art movements, which I reanalysed and reinterpreted in a modern context. This is what my new book is all about: art created with a connection to the past, free of common trends and stabilized taste.

It has been a very long and arduous journey, but finally here I am with a new publication. First of all I would like to thank Cunard for having given me the opportunity in 1994 to create original paintings for the 'Grand Old Lady of the Ocean', the glorious and legendary *QE2*. It was then that my relationship with the most famous cruise line in the world started. I wish to thank the former Cunard President and Managing Director Carol Marlow for her continuous support and for having allowed me and my team of assistants to return on the *QE2* during the summer of 2008 to restore my murals prior to the ship's final departure to the port of Dubai where she is now permanently docked.

Another thank you goes to the new President and Managing Director of Cunard, Mr. Peter Shanks, who enthusiastically welcomed my paintings and allowed me to continue my artistic legacy with Cunard Lines. I would also like to extend my gratitude to the interior design team of the *Queen Elizabeth* who appreciated the elegance of my style and prominently placed my paintings on the ship.

I must mention Rebecca Money, Managing Director of Ocean Books for her continuous support and for introducing my publication 'The Art of Giancarlo Impiglia', published by Rizzoli International Publishers in 1995, a 30 year retrospective, to the Cunard ships' libraries. Featured within it are reproductions of the paintings I created for the QE2 in 1994. It was Rebecca who introduced me to Miles Cowsill, publisher and editor-in-chief of Lily Publications, who also deserves many thanks for having decided to put in print a new book featuring not only my paintings created for the four Queens, but also my earliest paintings, from when I was a young artist in my native Rome. He also decided to include my most recent works which are presented in a new and comprehensive light. Thank you to Nicola Greene who supervised the production of the book and the talented Ian Smith who designed the book with his elegant taste and finally to Sara Donaldson the copy-editor who reviewed and corrected the script.

I am proud to say that my sons, Thomas and Christopher have been incredibly influential in the creation of my body of work. Thomas, now an architect, has inspired me with his exquisite taste in design, producing aesthetically beautiful projects since his teenage years. Christopher, his younger brother, has continued to motivate me, becoming the author of a successful epic poem 'The Song of The Fall' at the early age of 17. He furthermore graciously decided to write the introduction of this book. What more could I ask for?

To conclude this long list of collaborators who made this publication possible I must present the highest and warmest thank you to my wife Nina who, for all the years of our very long relationship, has never hesitated to support my creativity in spite of all the odds that an artist encounters on the way to success.

Giancarlo Impiglia

Plates (page number precedes title)

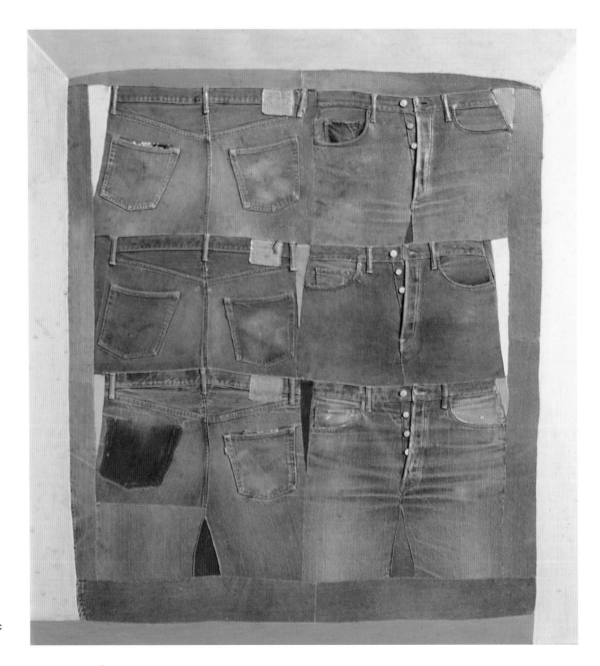

Three Body Buddies, 1967
Assemblage mounted on
canvas fabric, enamel, acrylic
and gold leaf, 58" x 61"

8

INTRODUCTION

One cannot help but be immersed in the brilliant colours and elegant lines of Giancarlo Impiglia's work. His bold canvases, dynamic drawings and vivacious hand-cut sculptures not only form a stunning reliving of the nostalgic Roaring 20s and 30s with numerous settings including the nightlife of New York City, the most popular clubs of Paris or Rome or the shores of the Riviera, they also contain relevant commentary on both contemporary values and on the social/political spheres of the modern world.

His paintings represent society's preoccupation with colourful materialism, the superficial quality of people's attire being the definition of their individual identity. Their costumes act as a beautiful facade under which they hide their true selves and their hidden desires. Their elegant exteriors are but satires of their genuine inner qualities. They are thus faceless and indifferent to each other, defined entirely by the folds of their gowns and the glitter of their jewellery.

Although based in New York, Impiglia is a native of Rome, where he studied at the Liceo Artistico and the Accademia di Belle Arti di Roma, working under some of the most important Italian post-war artists such as Umberto Mastroianni and Mario Mafai. He then went on to study photography and cinema at the Instituto Tecnico Fotografico "Duca D'Aosta" and at the Centro Italiano Addestramento Cinematografico.

As a young artist in his native Rome, Impiglia was part of the avant-garde of the early 60s participating in the Arte Povera movement, pioneered by artists such as Alberto Burri. These were memorable bohemian years during which he produced a large collection of assemblages in which he combined real blue jeans and various other pieces of clothing and fabrics including camouflage canvas, symbolizing the modern world's basic costume and calling out against the Vietnam War and social status. The use of camouflage is something Impiglia has continued to incorporate into his work, emphasizing his concept of the costume while hinting at people's natural inclinations towards violence.

After his participation in the Arte Povera movement, Impiglia proposed, in a constant evolution of technique and composition, the revival of art deco, the eclectic style which had remained dormant since WWII and was reawakened by Impiglia in the late 60s. Impiglia has since established a signature style recognizable throughout the world which has continued to expand into new creative visions.

Impiglia's work was no doubt drastically affected by his first visit to New York City in 1971. There the majestic skyline, bright lights and constant bustle of people and traffic brought a futurist vigour and energy to his work reminiscent of Giacomo Balla, Gino Severini and Umberto Boccioni, three of the major exponents of the Italian Futurist Movement of the early years of the 20th Century.

He had originally been brought to New York to perform as a musician. Since his teenage days at the Academy of Fine Arts in Rome he had been supporting his artistic endeavours by playing in nightclubs throughout Europe, from Tunisia to England, alongside some of the most famous performers of the day. For two decades he was thus exposed to the superficial glitz and glamour of urban nightlife which he then began to project onto the canvas.

It was in New York that Impiglia's unique style truly came into being, the culmination of his classical education and his study of Cubism and Futurism, his experience as a musician and the impact of modernity on his psyche. There his successful American and eventual international art career was launched. In 1974 he was commissioned to create a 60 x 6 foot mural for the lobby of the Great American Insurance Building at 99 John Street in New York City where the artist revisited the Works Progress Administration (WPA) period in a contemporary context. Using his eclectic style, Impiglia harked back to the period when America was emerging from the Great Depression, and the WPA was granting work to millions of unskilled and impoverished people. The Federal Art Project (FAP) was the visual arts branch of the WPA, sponsoring the creation of numerous public art works and stimulating the careers of artists such as Jackson Pollock and Diego Rivera.

Café Society Mural (detail),
1987
Five panels, acrylic on canvas,
each, 84" x 84", total 35' x 7'

The 99 John Street mural received great praise, propelling Impiglia's work across the United States and abroad in countless galleries, magazines, private collections and films. His 1987 commission for a 35 foot-long mural for Cafe Society, a famous nightclub on 21st Street and Broadway, was featured in the Hollywood hits *Big* featuring the young Tom Hanks and *Boomerang* alongside the comedian Eddie Murphy. Other iconic Impiglia images have graced the covers of Alberto Moravia's 1990 book *Le Ambizioni Sbagliate*, Norman Mailer's 1991 book *Deer Park*, and his style reached a truly global audience when his painting *Absolut Impiglia* became one of the official advertisements for Absolut Vodka.

His distinctive style led, in the 1990s, to his long-time relationship with Cunard, which continues to this day. In 1994, Impiglia received an unexpected phone call from Mr. John Olsen, President of Cunard Line, who wished to arrange a meeting to discuss a possible commission for the then under renovation *Queen Elizabeth 2*. Impiglia, although not yet acquainted with the ship's history, promptly accepted, taking a large portfolio of sketches, prints and original drawings to the meeting.

Mr. Olsen was already quite familiar with Impiglia's work, having seen the Cafe Society mural, with which he was deeply impressed. It was clear how Impiglia's style rang in perfect tune with the elegance and grandeur of the cruise liners of the past, from the *Titanic* to the *Normandie* and the first *Queen Mary*, a legacy which Cunard Line proudly continues. Impiglia's work would help fulfil Cunard's intentions to create an ambience which echoed the golden age of these cruise liners, but in a new and exciting colourful manner.

As a subject for the commission, it was suggested Impiglia depict an image of the famous Henley Regatta. The subject matter was indeed suitable, as the Regatta not only tied into the nautical theme, but also served as a quintessential British event representing royal patronage.

The resulting commission was a painting, Impiglia's own imaginative rendering of the Henley Regatta for the Lido bar, as well as two large canvases measuring 12 x 5 feet for the Lido promenades depicting a leisurely day onboard the vessel; in the paintings the captain looks on as figures enjoy the sunshine, play shuffleboard, swim in the pool or read a book while waiters serve tea. The paintings are truly evocative of the bygone era of F. Scott Fitzgerald, Salvador Dali and Pablo Picasso, casting the viewer back to the first half of the 20th century. Impiglia's work for Cunard continued when eighteen beautifully framed graphics were chosen to adorn the new Lido.

Due to the positive responses, by passengers and personnel alike, for Impiglia's *QE2* paintings, a new commission was proposed to the artist. In 2003 he was offered the opportunity by Cunard to create four paintings for the *Queen Mary 2*, the largest ocean liner ever built. Impiglia enthusiastically accepted the commission and created four paintings on the theme of entertainment which were eventually installed on Staircase B in front of the entrance to the magnificent Royal Court Theatre. The paintings, in Impiglia's distinguishable style, are impossible to miss.

The first painting depicts two couples dancing enthusiastically; in the second a lavishly dressed couple twirl on the dance floor to the sounds of a big band; in the third a couple has a romantic evening serenaded by a violin player; the fourth depicts the elegant cocktail hour onboard. All convey to the viewer the sensation of living during the time when crossing the ocean in style was the privilege of the few.

In 2007, with the construction of the new Cunarder, the *Queen Victoria*, Impiglia undertook a different artistic approach to harmonize with the romantic interior design scheme. He thus returned to his classical roots, demonstrating his ability as an adept draughtsman in the creation of a full-length portrait of Queen Victoria as a young woman. Working from a painting by a court artist depicting the Queen at the age of 22 or 23, Impiglia recreated the style of the mid-1800s when Victoria was the British monarch. He did so with pastels, a medium he prizes for its freshness of colour, and used them to create a chiaroscuro technique in imitation of the Renaissance masters. The intricately worked silk dress, delicately placed golden crown and gently held rose all blend seamlessly with the elegant majesty of the Queen's Room onboard.

With the 2008 relocation of the *QE2* to Dubai after more than 40 years of service, Cunard began the construction of its new ocean liner, the *Queen Elizabeth*. Impiglia, after a 15 year relationship with the Queens, was invited to create three original paintings and two original serigraphs which now adorn the new ship. The paintings stay true to the artist's style and palette but also remain strongly influenced by the modern art deco setting of the glamorous first *Queen Mary*. They are a worthy new chapter to Impiglia's long legacy on the Queens.

The three original paintings were created at the same time, ensuring that they remained in harmony with each other. The first painting depicts a formal evening in the dining room, in which the artist included the recreated image of a tapestry present on the first *Queen Mary* in which a mermaid rides four sea horses. In the second painting elegantly dressed guests descend the grand staircase on their way to the theatre. The third painting portrays a night of entertainment as a couple enjoys the sounds of a jazz band.

His work on the high seas has never been exclusively limited to his commissioned artworks. Since the early 1990s he has also been a guest lecturer onboard many cruise lines including Cunard, Seabourn, Silver Seas, Celebrity and Crystal Cruises. For Impiglia, teaching has always been extremely close to the heart, as it allows him to share his knowledge not only of his own work and experiences as an artist, but also his enthusiasm for the broader topic of art history. He has thus delivered numerous talks on various interesting subjects. These include the Sistine Chapel by Michelangelo, the Hermitage Collection in St. Petersburg, the Ancient Mosaics of Hagia Sophia in Istanbul, the

The Henley Regatta (detail),
1994
Acrylic on canvas, 99" x 36"

13

Ballroom (detail), 2003
Acrylic and gold leaf on
honeycomb aluminium panel,
48" x 72"

Excavations of Pompeii, the Birth of Modern Art, the History of Impressionism and the
Life and Work of Pablo Picasso.

In his most recent art works, Impiglia presents a new theme based on a rejuvenated
interest in ancient history. This, he claims, has evolved from his early exposure to history as
a boy growing up in Rome, expanding due to his more recent travels around the world and
his rediscovery of numerous ancient sites. These paintings depict duels of medieval crusaders
and imaginary portraits of venerable emperors, all in his hard-edged and complex style. The
modern treatment of these ancient soldiers ties together the unbroken timeline of religious
and political conflicts, especially in the Middle East, from centuries past to today's ongoing
turmoil. They suggest the powerful notion that although countless years have passed and
people have evolved, many aspects of the world have still not changed for the better.

Despite having forged a career largely in America, Impiglia's art has never been far

from home, and although many of his images present the cityscapes of an American metropolis, they nevertheless remain linked to the artist's Italian heritage and classical education. Remove the modern clothing and neon signs, replace the steel building facades with hand-cut stone covered in ivy; the colours, pose and composition of the figures and the layering of light and shade remain true to any great Italian Renaissance master from Giotto to Botticelli.

In his recent work this has become increasingly visible as Impiglia has also revisited the true classical style with intricate pencil sketches of Michelangelo's *David* and a life-size icon of St Sebastian on a backdrop of radiant gold leaf. The latter was greatly influenced by Giovanni Bellini, one of Impiglia's favourite painters of the Italian Renaissance, however Impiglia reinterprets the image as a symbol of human suffering in a world driven by greed, symbolized by the gold leaf.

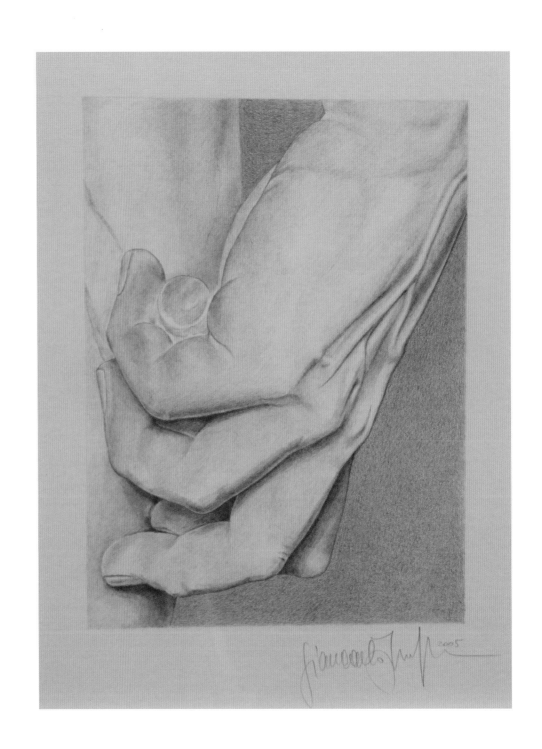

*David's Right Hand
(after Michelangelo), 2005*
Pencil and colour pencil on
board, 8¼" x 11½"

16

Unfortunately many modern artists have lost touch with the origins of their trade, when paintings attempted to capture the reality of the natural world around them with all of its energy and movement, whether this be the dense chiaroscuro of Caravaggio or the elegant lines of the Chauvet cave drawings in Southern France. Impiglia's keen interest in history and tight ties to his roots in the Eternal City have ensured such traditions have not been forgotten, demonstrating that they still have a major role to play in the formation of the modern artist.

Impiglia continues to demonstrate his unique artistic identity and his refusal to follow the rules of the art market, which dictate fashion and trends, instead working according to his own insight and interests.

Today his work is featured in the permanent collections of the Museum of the City of New York, the Zimmerli Art Museum at Rutgers University in New Jersey, the Kentucky Derby Museum, the Sangre de Cristo Arts Center in Pueblo, Colorado, the Italian American Museum of New York, the Pfizer Inc. art collection, the Absolut Art Collection in Stockholm, Sweden, the Victoria and Albert Museum in London, and many other institutions and private collections world wide.

Two books tracing Giancarlo Impiglia's career have been published by Rizzoli International: *Giancarlo Impiglia: Recent Work* with an introduction by Stephen Di Lauro in 1982 and *The Art of Giancarlo Impiglia,* a lavish overview of the artist's work from 1968 to 1994 with text by art critic and curator Ronny Cohen in 1995. The latter contains over 100 images including drawings, paintings, sculptures and assemblages.

This new book presented by Lily Publications is the fulfilment of Giancarlo Impiglia's very long and successful artistic career up to date. The images reproduced here are only a glimpse of the artist's massive portfolio, which demonstrates the phenomenal talent of a true Renaissance man, and which, for more than 50 years, has given joy and pleasure to art lovers around the world.

Christopher Impiglia

www.giancarloimpiglia.com   gimpiglia@gmail.com

My Dream, 1957
Oil on wood, 15" x 11"

18

My Father's Town, 1958
Oil on burlap, 39" x 27"

Above:
Poppies, 1958
Oil on wood, 15" x 28"

Right:
Untitled, 1958
Oil on wood, 15" x 28"

20

Still Life (homage to Giorgio Morandi), 1958
Oil on wood, 11" x 9"

Memories of Private Cantrell,
1967
Assemblage on canvas, blue
jeans, camouflage fabric,
58" x 72"

22

Mass Movement, 1968
Assemblage, blue jeans and
fabric mounted on canvas,
96" x 68"

Bowling
(after Michelangelo), 1973
Assemblage on canvas, blue
jeans, acrylic, red chalk,
36" x 48"

24

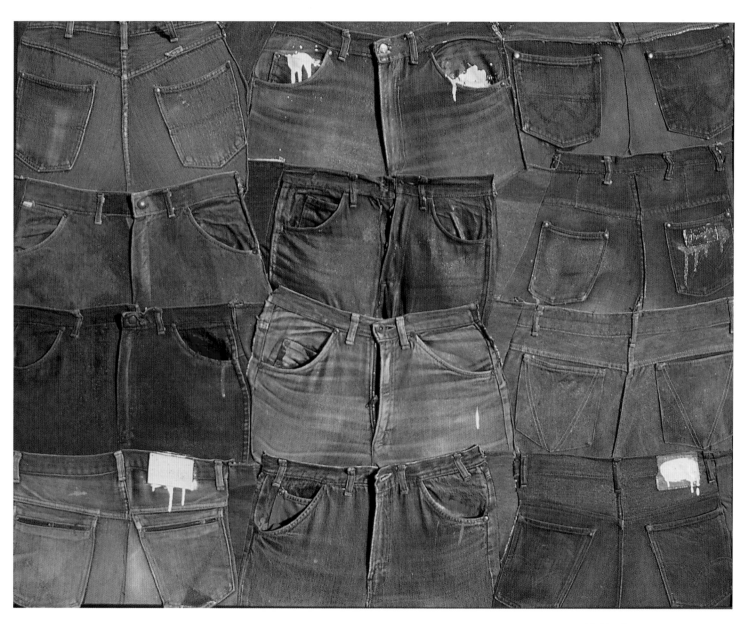

Multitude, 1973
Assemblage mounted on
canvas, blue jeans, acrylic
paint, 55" x 44"

Standing Group, 1973
Acrylic on assemblage
mounted on canvas, 68" x 60"

*Revisiting Lower Manhattan –
Mural 1975*
Lobby of 99 John Street
Central panel, acrylic on
canvas, 204" x 68"

Revisiting Lower Manhattan
(99 John Street), 1975
Left panel, acrylic on canvas,
156" x 68"

*Revisiting Lower Manhattan
(99 John Street), 1975*
Right panel, acrylic on canvas,
156" x 68"

99 John Street Mural,
work in progress, 1975
New York City

Mechanical Bird, 1979
Acrylic, enamel and gold leaf
on wood, 84" x 40" x 20"

The Tree of Geometry, 2000
Acrylic, enamel and gold leaf
on wood 117" high

The Tree of Geometry, 2000
Acrylic, enamel and gold leaf
on wood 117" high

33

Sculptures on rooftop, 1976
New York

34

Checking In, 1980
Acrylic on canvas, 48" x 54"

View of the studio, 1980
New York City

West 42nd Street, 1980
Acrylic on canvas, 60" x 71"

Flying High, 1981
Acrylic on canvas, 46" x 78"

Queuing
(study for a painting), 1981
Pencil on vellum, 64½" x 32"

Next Time, 1982
Acrylic on canvas, 24" x 30"

Stars and Stripes
(The Politician), 1982
Acrylic on canvas, 32" x 36"

Sunday Morning View (study),
1982
Pencil and pastel on vellum,
11¾" x 7¾"

Sunday Morning View, 1982
Acrylic on canvas, 72" x 48"

The Seductive Tube, 1982
Acrylic on canvas, 38" x 46"

Café Society (mural), 1987
Acrylic on canvas, 30' x 7'

Two details of Café Society.

Above: *The Big Band, 1987*
Acrylic on canvas, 84" x 84"

Right: *The Performance, 1987*
Acrylic on canvas, 84" x 84"

Backgammon Players, 1988
Pastel on board, 33" x 28"

Night Rhythm, 1988
Pastel on black paper,
46" x 84"

Butler With Tray, 1990
Acrylic on canvas, 36" x 78"

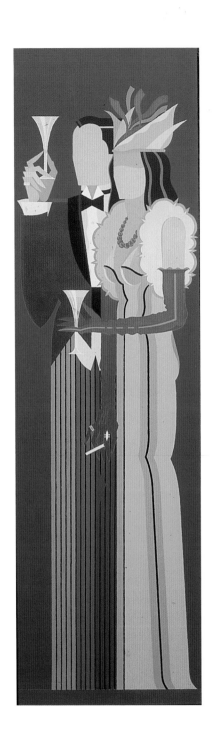

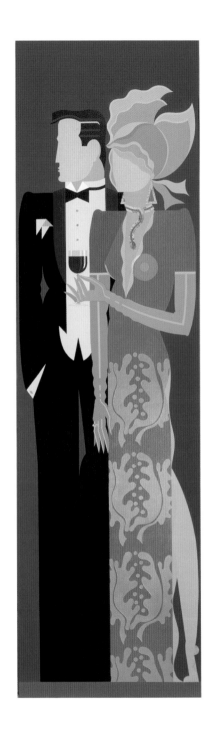

Left:
Champagne Toast, 1990
Acrylic on panel, 24" x 84"

Right:
Wine Toast, 1990
Acrylic on panel, 24" x 84"

Going Shopping, 1990
Acrylic on canvas, 37" x 51"

Party On The Grass,
Napa Valley, California, 1990
Seven life size sculptures,
acrylic on wood

Napa Cabernet, 1991
Acrylic on canvas, 52" x 69"

Tube Station, 1992
Pastel on board, 26½" x 47"

'1913', 1991
Acrylic and gold leaf on wood,
life-size, front and back views

55

Absolut Impiglia, 1992
Acrylic and gold leaf on panel,
31" x 33"
Commission for Absolut Vodka

Station, 1991
Acrylic on canvas, 48" x 48"

Night On Broadway, 1993
Pencil on vellum, 10" x 12"

Camouflage People, 1994
Acrylic and gold leaf on
camouflage fabric, 27" x 33"

Lifestyle I, 1994
Acrylic on canvas, 144" x 68". Commission for *QE2*

Lifestyle I, 1994
Pencil on vellum, study for
QE2 commission, 144" x 68"

Lifestyle II, 1994
Pencil on vellum, study for
QE2 commission, 144" x 68"

Lifestyle II, 1994
Acrylic on canvas,
144" x 68"
Commission for *QE2*

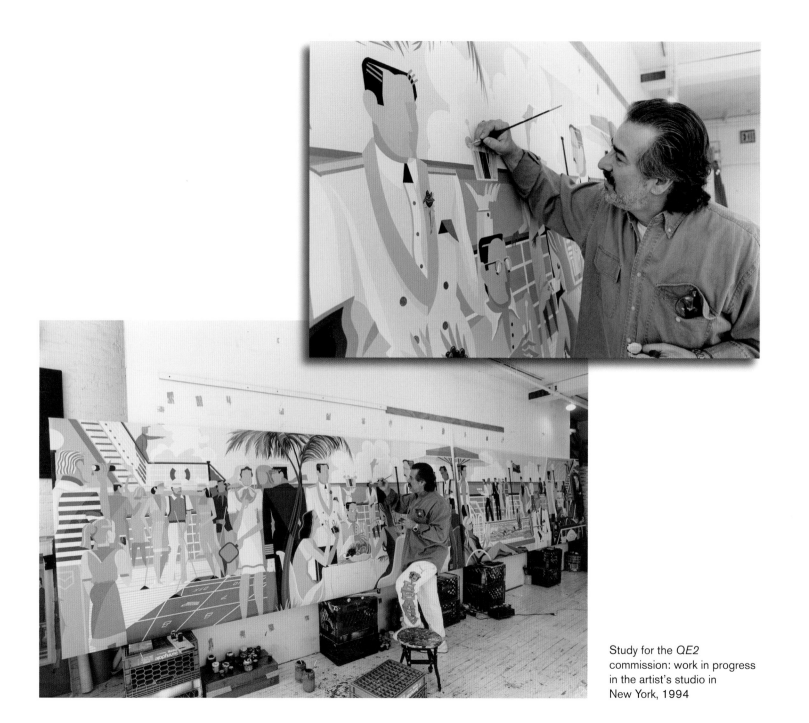

Study for the *QE2* commission: work in progress in the artist's studio in New York, 1994

Murals for the *QE2*:
work in progress in the artist's
studio
New York, 1994

The Henley Regatta, 1994
Pencil on vellum,
98½" x 35½"
Study for *QE2* commission

Henley Regatta, 1994
Acrylic on canvas, 98½" x 35½"
Commission for *QE2*

Queen Elizabeth 2

You are cordially invited to meet artist Giancarlo Impiglia
and view his latest works
Lifestyles I • Lifestyles II • Henley Regatta

Reception on board Queen Elizabeth 2
Two o'clock in the afternoon, Friday, January 6, 1995

New York Passenger Ship Terminal, West 55th Street at 12th Avenue, New York City

Please R.S.V.P. to Ms. Shari Aponte, 754.6500

Lifestyles I (Detail) ©1994 Giancarlo Impiglia

Front and back of invitation to
unveiling of murals on board
the *QE2*, 1995

69

The QE2 Whirlpool, 2001
Pencil and colour pencil on
paper, 20" x 18"

The QE2 Whirlpool II, 2001
Pencil on paper

Cocktail Hour, 2003
Acrylic and gold leaf on
honeycomb aluminium panel,
39" x 39"
Commission for the
Queen Mary 2

Moonlight Serenade, 2003
Acrylic and gold leaf on
honeycomb aluminium panel,
39" x 39"
Commission for the
Queen Mary 2

Showtime, 2003
Acrylic and gold leaf on
honeycomb aluminium panel,
48" x 72"
Commission for the
Queen Mary 2

Ball Room, 2003
Acrylic and gold leaf on
aluminium panel, 48" x 72"
Commission for the
Queen Mary 2

Performance at Sea, 2010
Coloured pencil on vellum,
96" x 61"
Study for the *Queen Elizabeth*
commission

*Study for Formal Evening in
the Queen Elizabeth Dining
Room, 2010*
Pencil on vellum, 60" x 40"
Commission for the
Queen Elizabeth

Study in color for Formal Evening in the Queen Elizabeth Dining Room, 2010
Coloured pencil on vellum,
60" x 40"
Commission for the
Queen Elizabeth

*Formal Evening in the Queen
Elizabeth Dining Room, 2010*
Acrylic on canvas, 60" x 40"
Commission for the
Queen Elizabeth

79

*Formal Evening In The Queen
Elizabeth Dining Room
(detail), 2010*
Acrylic on canvas, 60" x 40"
Commission for the
Queen Elizabeth

Queen Elizabeth paintings in progress, 2010

*Dancing In The Queen's
Room, 2010*
Acrylic on canvas, 40" x 30"
Commission for the
Queen Elizabeth

*Dancing In The Queen's
Room (detail), 2010*
Acrylic on canvas, 40" x 30"
Commission for the
Queen Elizabeth

Guests Descending The
Grand Staircase, 2010
Acrylic on canvas, 40" x 30"
Commission for the
Queen Elizabeth

84

*Guests Descending The
Grand Staircase (detail), 2010*
Acrylic on canvas, 40" x 30"
Commission for the
Queen Elizabeth

Girl with the Yellow Robe,
1986
Acrylic on canvas, 48" x 58"

Mistress, 1986
Acrylic on canvas, 48" x 54"

People Come And Go, 1995
Life-size sculpture,
acrylic on wood

88

La Commedia Dell'Arte,
homage to Gino Severini,
1998
Acrylic on canvas, 32" x 28"

The Premier (work in progress), 1998
Pencil and colour pencil on vellum, 16¼" x 21½"

The Premier, 1998
Acrylic on canvas, 60" x 66"

In The Tube, 1998
Acrylic on canvas, 68" x 48"

Cityscape, 1998
Oil on tar paper, 24" x 18"

Grape Picker, 1999
Acrylic on camouflage fabric

94

Night Crowd, 1999-2000
Acrylic on canvas, 56" x 80"

Chinatown, 1999-2000
Oil on panel, 96" x 48"

Fragments Of Landscape,
2000
Acrylic on canvas,
43½" x 61½"

Hector and Andromache,
Homage To Giorgio De
Chirico, 2000
Acrylic on cut out aluminium,
48" x 84"

Above:
The Muse Of Architecture,
Homage To De Chirico, 2001
Oil on canvas, 30" x 48"

Left:
Bodies In Conflict, 2002
Oil on panel, 30" x 40"

99

The Escalator, 2000
Acrylic on cut out aluminium,
48" x 81"

100

The Garden of Eden, 2001
Acrylic on tar paper, 42" x 22"

Ritmo Plastico, 2000
Acrylic on canvas, 40" x 50"

Geometry Of Nature I, 2002
Acrylic and gold leaf on cut
out honeycomb aluminium,
89" x 62"

Geometry Of Nature II, 2002
Acrylic, enamel and gold leaf
on cut out honeycomb
aluminium, 84" x 72"

Body In Lingerie, 2002
Oil on wood, 26" x 31"

The Sins Of Eve, 2002
Oil on cut out honeycomb
aluminium, 72" x 68"

Supernova, 2005
Oil on canvas, 84" x 72"

Specter I, 2005
Oil on canvas, 36" x 36"

Specter II, 2005
Oil on canvas, 36" x 36"

Summer Nudes, 2009
Oil on canvas, 16" x 16"

Constantinople 1453, 2011
Oil on canvas, 60" x 72"
Book cover for 'The Song of
the Fall', an epic poem by
Christopher Impiglia

Above:
*Study For The Fallen Warrior,
2011*
Black ink on vellum, 18" x 20"

Right:
The Fallen Warrior, 2011
Oil on canvas, 8" x 10"

The Battle Of Constantinople,
2011
Oil on canvas, 10" x 8"

The Crusader, 2011
Acrylic on canvas, 8" x 10"

114

The Emperor's Ghost, 2011
Acrylic on camouflage fabric,
30" x 40"

Above:
Brocade, 2011
Acrylic on brocade fabric,
59" x 49"

Right:
Personaggi, 2011
Acrylic on camouflage fabric,
36" x 46"

Above:
Bicycle Riders, 2011
Oil on canvas, 18" x 24"

Left:
Untitled painting, 2011
Oil on canvas, 24" x 18"

Untitled II, 2011
Oil on canvas, 24" x 18"

Vortex, 2011
Oil on canvas, 18" x 16"

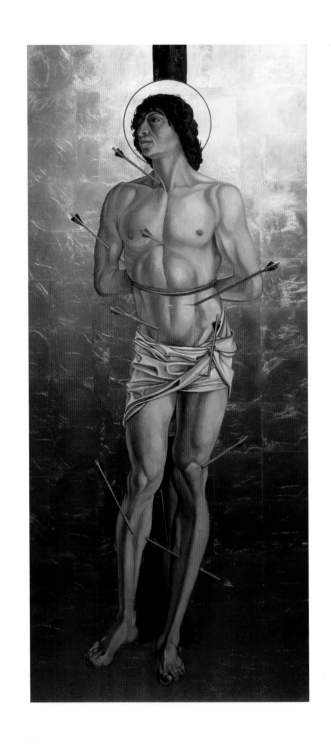

St Sebastian,
(after Giovanni Bellini), 2012
Oil and gold leaf on panel,
37" x 72"